DISCARD

IF YOU WERE A
CAT

Clare Hibbert

A+

Smart Apple Media

Published in the United States by Smart Apple Media
PO Box 3263, Mankato, Minnesota 56002

Editor: Joe Harris
Picture researcher: Clare Hibbert
Designer: Emma Randall

Picture credits:
All images Shutterstock except 8t Michael Weber/Imagebroker/FLPA, 12b Konrad Wothe/Imagebroker/FLPA, 20b PICANI/Imagebroker/FLPA, 26-27 Kerstin Luhrs/Tierfotoagentur/FLPA.

Library of Congress Cataloging-in-Publication Data

Hibbert, Clare, 1970-
 If you were a cat / Clare Hibbert.
     p. cm. -- (If you were a--)
 Audience: Grade 4 to 6.
 Summary: "Describes the features, life, and habits of cats in contrast to human life"-- Provided by publisher.
 Includes bibliographical references and index.
 ISBN 978-1-59920-959-3 (library binding)
 1. Cats--Juvenile literature. 2. Cats--Behavior--Juvenile literature. I. Title. II. Title: Cat.
 SF445.7.H533 2014
 636.8--dc23
                           2013002949

Printed in China

Supplier 03, Date 0513, Print Run 2367
SL002497US

Contents

How Cats Hunt

If you were a cat, you would be an expert hunter—just like your wild cousins, lions and tigers. With your sneaky stalking skills and lethal claws, you could catch and kill rats, mice, and birds. You might also prey on worms, frogs, or snakes, and chase butterflies for fun.

Hunting Technique
Cats creep up on their prey, keeping low to the ground. Just before they pounce, they check their balance with a wiggle of their bottom. They grip the victim with their claws and deliver a killer bite to the neck.

Playing with Food
Cats do not always kill prey outright. You might see a cat batting a mouse to and fro. This behavior may look cruel, but it is just the cat's way of checking that the mouse is no longer able to escape.

Cat Questions

Q: Why does my cat bring in live mice?
A: Mother cats bring their kittens live prey so they can practice hunting. Your pet might be trying to teach another cat in the household—or it might be trying to teach you!

Caring for Claws

Cats' claws are sheathed in a protective covering, so that walking does not blunt them. When cats scrape their claws down a tree trunk, they are scratching away the worn, outer layers to reveal new, sharp tips.

Cats' Eyes

If you were a cat, you would have extraordinary eyesight. You would make use of all of your senses when hunting, but sight would be especially important. You could spot prey from three football fields away, and you would even be able to see in the dark, too.

Hunter's Eyes

Cats have large eyes that let in lots of light. They can see six times better than humans in dim light. Like other predators, they have binocular ("two-eyed") vision, which means that they focus on objects with both eyes at once.

Cat Questions

Q: Why do cats' eyes reflect a flashlight?
A: Cats have a reflective "mirror" at the back of their eyes. This helps them to see in the dark, by bouncing light back over the retina, the part of their eyes that senses light.

Eye Colors

Cats' eyes come in many colors. They may be shades of blue, green, and brown—or even orange or yellow. The prize for the strangest pair goes to the Odd-Eyed White Persian, with one blue eye and one orange.

Clear View

Cats have a cloudy-looking extra eyelid or membrane that stops their eyes from drying out. It sweeps across the eyes when they blink, spreading moisture. If the membrane stays across, however, the cat could be sick and should be taken to a veterinary surgeon.

Amazing Senses

If you were a cat, you would rely on all your amazing senses, not only sight. You would have keen hearing to detect the faintest rustling and a nose that could read other cats' scent messages. You would also have sensitive whiskers to tell you more about your surroundings.

Sound Catchers

Cats' ears are large and mobile (able to move). They can turn toward a sound and figure out where it is coming from. Cats can hear high-pitched sounds, such as mouse squeaks, outside the range of human hearing.

Cat Questions

Q: Who can taste better—me or my cat?
A: Experts used to think cats could only detect meaty and fatty flavors. Now we know their sense of taste is more complex. Still, cats have fewer than 475 taste buds, whereas humans have around 9,000!

Smell Power

Cats' sense of smell is 14 times better than humans'. However, unlike dogs, cats do not track prey by smell. A special organ on the roof of the mouth picks up scents. Sometimes they gape (open their mouths wide) to smell better.

Facial Feelers

Cats have whiskers on their face and wrists. Whiskers sense movements in the air, allowing cats to build up a picture of their surroundings. They help cats to avoid obstacles and to pinpoint their prey.

Contented Cats

If you were a cat, you would have many ways to communicate. You would use body language, facial expressions, scents, and your voice. You would be able to make a range of different noises. These would let humans and other cats know when you were feeling content.

Purring

Cats respond to things that make them happy with a rumbling purr. They purr when their owner strokes them—or as kittens, when their mother feeds them milk. Between cats, a purr is a sign that there is no threat.

Cat Questions

Q: Why does my cat purr at the vet's?
A: When cats purr in anxious situations, they are not expressing contentment. They are trying to reassure themselves. Perhaps the sound helps them to feel safe because it reminds them of being a kitten.

Cat Greetings

Cats say "hello" with a warbling sound, sometimes called a "chirrup". They make this friendly noise to greet other cats. They also chirrup to their owners—the sound means "Welcome home!" or "I'm back!".

Talking Cat

One of the best-known cat noises is the meow. This is not just a greeting—it is how cats demand attention. Where the cat is will give clues to what it wants—most likely, it wants to be let in or out the door, or it wants to be fed.

Grumpy Cats

If you were a cat, you would not only use your voice to show when you were feeling friendly. You would also be able to speak your mind when you were feeling frightened or wanting to stand your ground. You could make all kinds of horrible howls and hisses.

Growling

When two cats are in a stand-off situation, they growl at each other from deep in the throat. Cats also growl if people get too close or try to hold them when they do not want to be held. The message is clear: "Back off!"

Fighting Cats

If neither cat is scared off by growls, a pair may fight to see who is "top cat". As they lash out with their sharp claws, fighting cats hiss, spit, snarl, and shriek. Hissing is a sign of feeling threatened.

Cat Questions

Q: Why can't pet cats roar?
A: Only lions, tigers, leopards, and jaguars can roar. These big cats have a special larynx (voice box) and a flexible throat bone that work together to create the roar.

Nasty Noises

Caterwauling is the nasty, screeching sound that cats sometimes make. Females do it to tell toms (males) in the neighborhood that they are ready to mate. Cats also howl if they are anxious, in pain, or simply want attention.

Body Language

If you were a cat, your body and face would speak volumes. Other cats—and people—would be able to tell if your mood was friendly or aggressive, just from the position of your ears or tail. How you held and moved your body would help you to communicate.

Angry or Fearful?

An angry cat will send warning signals before biting or scratching. To warn others to steer clear, the cat draws back its ears, narrows its eyes, and bares its teeth. Fearful cats flatten their ears, too, but they widen their eyes.

Tail Talk

When a cat is annoyed, it swishes its tail to and fro. This, like growling (see page 12), is the cat's way of saying "Go away!". When a cat is really afraid, it puffs out its tail and fur, so that its body looks bigger than it really is.

14

Cat Questions

Q: How can I tell if my cat wants to play?
A: Even fully grown cats can be kittenish and playful. Trail a piece of ribbon past the nose of a relaxed, sprawling cat. If its eyes open and its ears and whiskers perk up, it wants to play.

Walk Talk

Even the way a cat walks reveals something about its state of mind. Cats that are at ease walk tall with their tail held high in the air. Cats that are less sure of themselves will cower and hold their tail low to the ground.

15

The Home Range

If you were a cat, you would have your own territory, or home range. If you were a female or a neutered male, you might not venture beyond your own backyard. If you were a tom, you would roam farther and have a much larger territory.

Scent Messages

Cats use smell to mark their territory. They have scent glands on the muzzle, temples, and base of the tail. Rubbing these glands against surfaces, such as fence posts or plant pots, leaves behind a subtle scent.

Cat Questions

Q: How will my cat handle moving to a new house?
A: Moving can upset cats. It is best to keep them in one room at first, providing food, water, and a litter tray. After a week or so, they can go out—and establish their new territory.

Taking Over

Females and neutered males sometimes agree to share part of their territory, but toms do not. Old toms usually have a strong and sturdy body—and battle scars from all the fights they've taken part in to defend their range.

Spraying

Toms have a way to leave more powerful smell messages. They can back toward an object, tail held high, and then squirt foul-smelling urine. This is called spraying. Sometimes neutered males spray, too.

How Cats Move

If you were a cat, you would have an amazingly supple, or flexible, body. You could curl into a ball or lengthen your back in a superlong stretch. This flexibility would give you the edge when hunting—you could effortlessly climb and leap, sprint and pounce.

Climbing

Leopards, jaguars, and many other wild cats are at ease in the trees. Pet cats enjoy the safety of a treetop lookout, too. Climbing a tree trunk does not take too much effort, thanks to their light body and strong claws for gripping.

Supportive Skeleton

Like humans, cats have a backbone made up of vertebrae (smaller bones). Their bones are only loosely connected, so the spine is very bendy. Cats do not have a fixed collarbone under the neck, so the front legs are free to stretch forward.

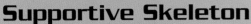

Cat Questions

Q: Why does my cat move in its sleep? Is it dreaming?

A: Cats spend two-thirds of their lives asleep. Like sleeping humans, they have different cycles of brain activity, including REM sleep, when dreaming occurs. Dreaming cats twitch and even swat imaginary prey!

Sense of Balance

Cats can walk along the narrowest ledges and fences. They practice their tightrope skills as kittens. If they fall, they almost always land on their feet. A balance organ in their ears helps them to steady themselves in midair.

19

Caring for Fur

If you were a cat, you would take pride in your coat of soft fur, which would protect your body from the cold and the heat. Its coloring and pattern might camouflage you and hide you from enemies or prey. If you were a pedigree cat, you might have been bred to have a special coat.

Staying Clean

Cats are constantly grooming. They run their rough, comblike tongue through the hairs to keep them clean and sleek. Cats use a licked paw as a washcloth to groom harder-to-reach places, such as the top of the head.

Shared Care

Cats are not pack animals like dogs, but they sometimes live in family groups. Cats from the same family may groom each other. This shows they trust each other and results in them having a shared "family smell".

Cat Questions

Q: Why does my cat scratch itself?
A: Scratching is a sign of having fleas—parasites that live in fur. Cats that go outside pick up flea eggs that have dropped off other cats. A vet can advise you on how to get rid of them.

Cat Diet

Most cats eat a combination of wet food, from cans and pouches, and dry food. The dry food helps to keep their teeth clean and their gums healthy. Cats enjoy fresh fish and meat, too.

Cat Questions

Q: Why do cats cough up slimy hairballs?
A: When a cat grooms, it ends up swallowing a lot of its own hair. About once a week, cats cough up hairballs, so that the hair does not build up in their stomach.

Kittens

If you were a kitten, you would need to stay with your mother for the first two or three months of your life. She would feed you milk, keep you warm and clean, and teach you the skills you would need to survive on your own as an adult cat.

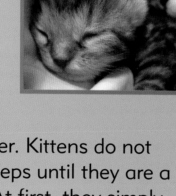

Newborns

A mother cat gives birth in a safe, cozy "nest". She usually has four babies in her litter. Kittens do not take their first steps until they are a few weeks old. At first, they simply wriggle, squirm, and snuggle up to their mom.

Milk

Kittens feed on their mothers' milk. The first milk, colostrum, gives extra protection against disease. Kittens make their mother produce milk by "kneading"—pushing with one paw at a time. Later in life, cats knead when they are contented.

Cat Questions

Q: Why are kittens always fighting?

A: At first, kittens only feed and sleep, but by about four weeks, they discover how to play—and how to play-fight. This is how they learn the skills for life as a hunter!

Kitten Senses

Kittens are born with their eyes and ears closed. Their main sense is smell. The kittens' eyes open a week or two later, but it takes a few days before they can focus. Kittens start to hear at two to three weeks old.

Cat Breeds

If you were a cat, you would be a distant relative of the African wildcat. Perhaps you would be a mongrel cat, or perhaps you would be a pedigree cat that belongs to a particular breed. People started developing breeds during the nineteenth century.

Tabby Markings

Most wild cats have spots, patches, and stripes on their coat, even if these only appear on the kittens. Many pet cats have these "tabby" markings, too. They provide camouflage in dappled light.

Cat Choices

Over time, people have bred cats for certain features. Today, there are more than a hundred cat breeds. Some are short-haired and some are long-haired; some are one color and some have multicolored markings.

On Display

Cat shows began nearly 150 years ago. People brought their pedigree cats to be judged, and the best examples of each breed won prizes. Of course, in any pet owner's opinion, the most perfect cat is their own!

Cat Questions

Q: Do all cats have fur?
A: Almost all cats have fur, but there is one hairless breed. The strange-looking Sphynx was developed for people who love cats but are allergic to their fur.

Humans and Cats

If you were a cat, you would be used to getting along with humans—after all, cats have been domesticated for thousands of years. You would rely on people to provide you with food and shelter. In return, you would offer companionship and possibly pest control (keeping mice away).

First Contact

Staring is threatening to cats. A human who wants to "make friends" should look away with eyes half-closed, occasionally blinking. Cats do not like a fuss—that is why they often head straight for whoever is ignoring them.

Fur Care

When cats groom each other, it is a sign of trust (see page 20). Grooming helps owners bond with their cats, too. Long-haired breeds need grooming every day, otherwise their fur becomes terribly tangled.

Health Care

As well as providing food, water, and safety, an owner needs to register their pet cat with a vet. The vet will provide the animal's medical care, treating it when it is sick and giving vaccinations to prevent disease.

Cat Questions

Q: Why should I have my cat neutered?
A: Neutering is an operation to remove the reproductive organs. It stops females from having unwanted kittens and helps to stop males from spraying (see page 17) and fighting.

Glossary

breed A class of cats that look similar and come from the same background.

carnivore An animal with a mostly meat diet.

colostrum The rich, first milk that a mammal mother produces after the birth of her offspring.

domesticated Describes an animal that is used to living alongside people, rather than in the wild.

gland A part of the body that produces a useful substance. Cats have scent glands that produce a smelly oil that they can use to leave scent messages.

guard hair One of the long, straight hairs that make up the top layer of a cat's coat.

membrane A thin, skinlike covering. Cats have a third eyelid called the nictitating membrane that spreads moisture across the eyes.

molt To lose old hair. This happens throughout the year to make way for new growth, but many animals also have a heavy molt in spring, when they thin down their thick winter coat.

mongrel A nonpedigree cat.

muzzle The part of an animal's face that sticks out, which includes the nose and mouth.

neutered Describes an animal that has had an operation to remove its reproductive organs so that it cannot have young.

organ A body part that has a particular function.

parasite An animal that lives on another animal and relies on it for food.

pedigree A cat of a particular breed, which has been registered with an official cat club.

prey An animal that is hunted by other animals for food. Mice and baby birds are typical prey for pet cats.

REM sleep Short for Rapid Eye Movement sleep, the part of the sleep cycle where sleep is lighter, not deep, and dreaming is more likely to occur.

reproductive organs The parts of the body involved in producing offspring.

sheathed Inside a protective covering.

spraying Producing a few quick squirts of smelly urine in order to mark territory.

taste buds Receptors in the mouth that send signals to the brain, which then makes sense of that information, allowing an animal to taste.

temple The part of the head between the forehead and the ear.

territory The area of land where an animal lives. Cats mark their territory by leaving their scent.

tom A male cat that has not been neutered.

vaccination An injection (shot) that helps the body to fight off a particular disease.

vitamin C A substance that helps animals to stay healthy. Cats produce their own vitamin C. Humans must take it in by eating plant foods.

Further Reading

Amazing Cat Facts and Trivia by Tammy Gagne (Chartwell Books, Inc., 2011)

Cats and Kittens (Get to Know Your Pet) by Jinny Johnson (Saunders Book Company, 2011)

How to Speak Cat by Sarah Whitehead (Scholastic Nonfiction, 2008)

Mini Encyclopedia: Cats by Sarah Creese (Make Believe Ideas, 2011)

Uncover a Cat by Paul Beck (Silver Dolphin, 2011)

Why Do Cats Have Whiskers? by Elizabeth MacLeod (Kids Can Press, 2008)

Web Sites

http://animal.discovery.com/cat-guide/
A guide to cat care from the Animal Planet web site, with information on kitten development, cat anatomy (how their bodies work), and interactive games to play.

http://animals.nationalgeographic.com/animals/mammals/domestic-cat/
National Geographic's guide to the domestic cat.

http://www.aspca.org/Home/Pet-care/cat-care
Information on how to care for your pet cat from the animal welfare charity, the ASPCA.

http://kids.cfa.org
A web site from the Cat Fanciers' Association with information on breeds, careers with cats, and also fun games to play.

http://www.saveacat.org
Information about saving abandoned cats from Alley Cat Rescue (ACR).

Index